STRONG GIRL SPIRIT
WITH GOD

21 DAYS OF PLANTING & GROWING SEEDS OF STRENGTH

THIS JOURNAL BELONGS TO

_ _ _ _ _ _ _ _ _ _ _ _ _ _ _ _ _ _ _

First Edition

Copyright © 2020 Terrie Nathan
Strong Girl Enterprises

www.terrienathan.com

All rights reserved.

ISBN: 978-1-7352766-0-1

No part of this book may be reproduced or transmitted in any form or by any means, electronic or mechanical, including photocopying, recording or by an information storage and retrieval system – except by a reviewer who may quote brief passages in a review to be printed in a magazine, newspaper or on the Web – without permission in writing from the publisher.

Design by Margaret Cogswell
margaretcogswell.com

i dedicate this book to all the strong women & men in my life.

The people that have inspired me and continue to inspire me every day with amazing support, strength, humor, beauty, and unconditional love.
YOU ALL HOLD THE TRUE SPIRIT OF STRENGTH!

Monica, my daughter,
Dean, my son,
my Mom,
my Dad,
Rylee & Desi, my granddaughters,
Mary, my daughter-in-law,
Haley, my stepdaughter,
Ian, my stepson,
Chris, my son-in-law,
Harley, my grandson,
Grandma Tina,
Grandma Ruby (the original Strong Girl),
and my biggest fan, soul-mate, and best friend,
my husband Eric.

a special note to the amazing parents of all the strong girls out there.

I'm sure you already know this,
but it is worth repeating, as repetition is our friend.

Children learn by example, by what we do, what we say, and who we are.

Our children are **always listening, always watching and always learning.**

You (Mom, Dad, Aunt, Uncle, Grandma, and Grandpa) are always on stage and **you take center stage in your child's world.**

Pay attention to your attitude and body language towards others, towards yourself & towards the world around you.

Answer your children's questions honestly. There is a "Strong Girl" in all girls. **Take an active role** in planting and growing the seeds of strength, acceptance, and respect in your Strong Girl.

Your show of strength about yourself is her model.

Every positive word you plant in your child needs watering and **you hold the water bucket.**

Help to reinforce these powerful words of strength, daily, in your Strong Girl.

Dear Strong Girl,

What you focus on grows!

Have you ever planted a seed in the ground? Even if you haven't, the only way the seed grows into a flower, or a vegetable or fruit, is to water it daily and to care for it.

We are the same, we are growing and learning every day, if we don't feed ourselves with daily positive thoughts, we won't grow and be the best we can be.

It takes practice, in the same way you learned to ride a bike, learned to walk, learned to play a sport or instrument, or even tie your shoes, it's the small, daily positive steps over and over again that build your daily habit of positive strength.

Positive words give life and the positive seeds you plant within yourself will begin to shape the way you see yourself and the world, in a good way.

Each day as you say it and pray it, you will become stronger and stronger. Each day you will be reminding yourself just how amazing you are.

But be careful, because just like a flower, sometimes weeds will get in the way. Sometimes our weeds are negative friends, family, bullies, and maybe even sometimes ourselves.

So, when the weeds of life around you start popping up, you will need to feed yourself with more positive seeds of strength.

There are two things we can control:
1. The way we feel, and
2. The way we think.

You can't control how someone else acts or behaves, just like you can't control if it rains or if it's sunny outside. You can only control how you feel about it and how you react to the situation at hand.

What you say affects how you live. You will be rewarded by how you speak
Proverbs 18:21 (ICB)

Strong Girls...
- - - - - - - -

Stand up for themselves

Take charge of how you feel

Reality check: Ask, "Does it really matter?"

Own it; own how you feel about it

Notice how you are feeling in the moment, acknowledge the feeling, and then choose to move on

Get your cape of confidence on...

You are the ONLY superhero you need. Put on your cape of confidence, you have the power to be YOU, be Confident, be strong!

There is beauty in strength of mind and thoughts, you've got this Strong Girl!

xoxo,
Terrie Nathan

How to Get the Most Out of This Daily Journey

Strong Girl, whatever you think about expands in your life.

When you think about your blessings, your many strengths, and the people you love and who love you, you will then attract many more blessings. Negative or discouraging thoughts do not simply go away, they must be replaced with positive and faith filled thoughts.

This sometimes can be a tough order, **that's why it takes daily practice.**

Building positive habits takes time, so over the next 21 days we will plant daily positive seeds in your life.

Along the way you will also be able to journal and log your thoughts to further add to your growth, motivation, and strength **with God.**

Daily Strong Girl motivation will put a smile on your face, in your heart, and in the hearts of others in your life.

Your light of strength will shine bright!
Empower ... Encourage ... Embrace your words.

"God made this day and I'm going to enjoy it and be happy!"
Psalm 118:24

– – – – – – – – –

Have you planted and prayed your "Strong Girl Seeds of Strength" today?

When you see 🪴 that means say it out loud.

The more you **say it and pray it** the stronger you will get.
Answer the questions, journal your thoughts, write down your feelings.

Use sticky notes to post in your room, or put on your mirror
or in your book. The more you **say it and pray it**, the more you will
grow and build your muscle of faith and positive thinking.

Finally, pass on the positive! Use the same stickers to plant seeds of strength
into someone else. Now go out and be the best version of you, Strong Girl.

– – – – – – – – –

When you see 🕊 that means Pray It.

SAY IT
Strength **A**biding **Y**ou Are Loved

PRAY IT
Practice **R**eceive **A**bundance and Jo**Y**

use your check in chart!

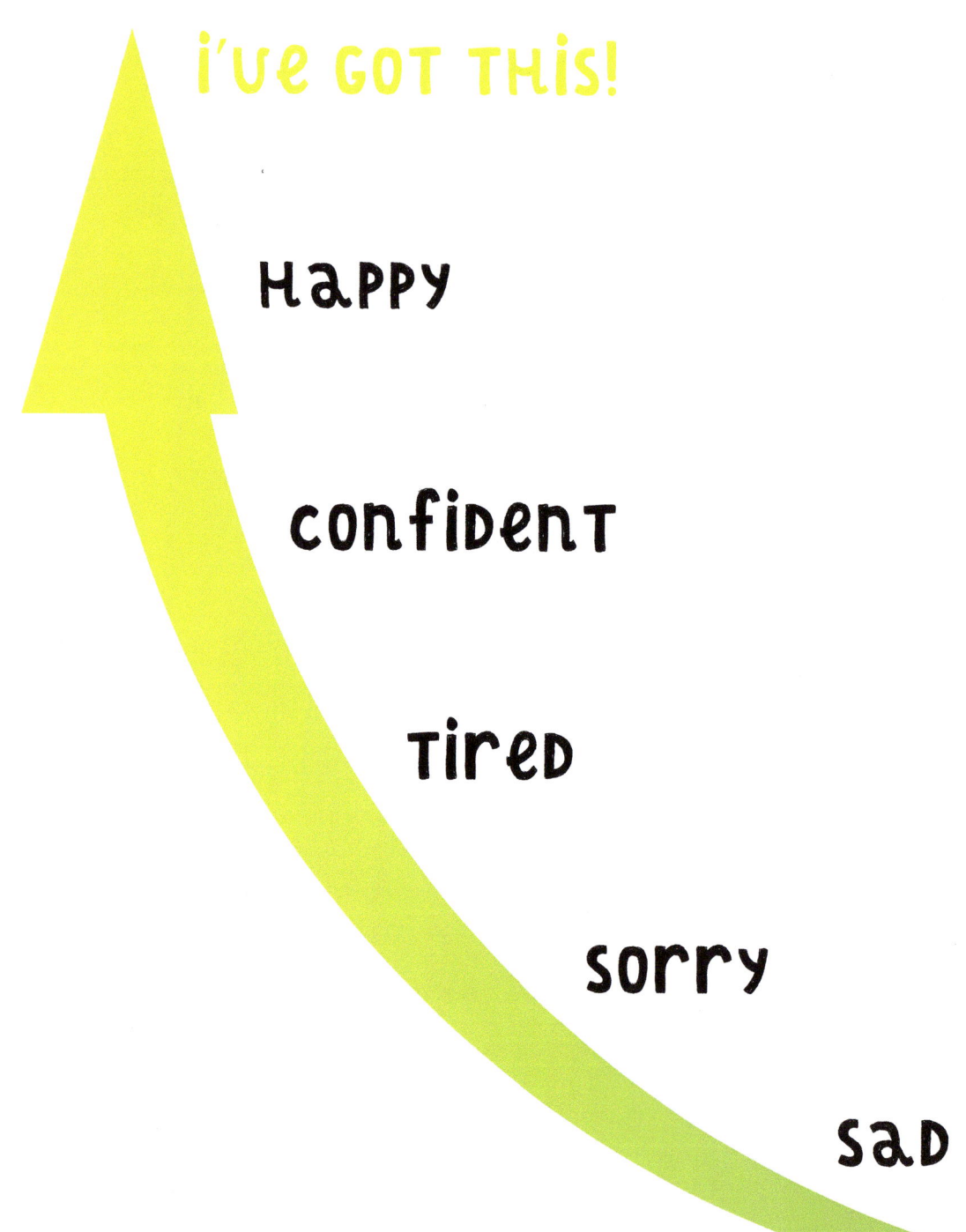

i've got this!

happy

confident

tired

sorry

sad

How are you feeling? What can you do to climb up the curve of strength? With God on your side, you've got this, Strong Girl!

excited

proud

silly

lonely

frustrated

mad

You're doing
GREAT!

You're making **MORE** of a difference than you REALIZE.

What you're going through is temporary. God will always make a way.

You're **ONE OF A KIND.** Trying to fit in is overrated, because you already fit **PERFECTLY** as you.

The world is
SO MUCH BETTER
because you're in it.

your **SMILE**
makes others smile.

Think **HAPPY THOUGHTS** today.

You are never **ALONE.**
Wherever you go and whatever you do,
GOD GOES WITH YOU.

God goes through everything
WITH YOU.

**SMILING
&
LAUGHING**
will lift your mood
and other's too.

You are
STRONGER
than you realize
and more
CAPABLE
than you know.

You have gifts that
ONLY YOU
can give this world.

Just so you know, God is **always** cheering you on.

are you ready to start your journey, strong girl?

GOOD MORNING, STRONG GIRL.
WELCOME TO
Day One

🕯️ SAY IT: I am amazing

God, help me to always remember that you made me special and that I am one of a kind. Thank you for making me unique. I have a special place in this world.
Amen.

🕊️ PRAY IT: I am amazing

You made my whole being. You formed me in my mother's body. I praise you because you made me in an amazing and wonderful way. What you have done is wonderful.
Psalm 139:13-14 ICB

THE MOST IMPORTANT THING A GIRL WEARS IS HER CONFIDENCE.

We are what we say we are ... you are amazing.
Dear Strong Girl, it is ok to be comfortable with who you are.
It's about being you and loving the AMAZING YOU that YOU are!
Now write two things that you think make you amazing.

_____

_____

Now the next step: while at school or church, while playing with friends, your brother, your sister, your mom, your dad, or the family pet, tell them why you think they are amazing.

Lessons Learned

I am amazing.

I can remember a time when I had to dress up for a special event at school. I didn't have much to pick from at the time, but I did have this one dress my grandma made for me.

When I showed up for the event, some girls starting laughing and asking me how I got that "dumb dress." All of the sudden I was so embarrassed to be wearing it. Just at that moment a teacher came by and whispered in my ear, "**You are amazing**, now just keep on saying it to yourself!" She said, "You can just erase those mean words with your pretend 'pink eraser.'" So I did. I erased them and then I kept running those three words, "you are amazing," through my mind.

It worked and I no longer felt stupid or ugly because I was wearing a dress others didn't like. I was so proud and happy that this dress I was wearing was a one of a kind dress. And in that moment I was Strong Girl. Those words have stuck with me.

I AM amazing and so are you!

If you don't like the words that are spoken to you, then change the words you speak to yourself. Choose words of positivity. Pull out your mental 'pink eraser' and erase the words that are not positive!

Trust me, it works.

Lessons Learned

I am strong.

We all want to fit in and to be like the cool kids. I know that's what I always wanted, was to just fit in, but it seemed I never could. But what does that mean, really?

Well, you know what? I am so glad that I was different, that I am different, and that I am cool in my own way. Being strong doesn't just mean to have strong muscles. Being strong means being strong in your thoughts. It means to be proud of who you are, love your flaws, love your quirks, love how your nose wrinkles when you smile. Be strong in self.

Because I didn't fit in as a young girl, I struggled to see my strength. I was very lucky as a young girl to have a grandma that spoke positive words of favor into my life. When I would visit her she would always tell me how beautiful, kind, and loving I was. She always called me her Strong Girl and would ask me who I was, and I would respond, "I AM Strong Girl."

These positive words have stuck with me and continue to move me through days, even when I am struggling with something.

Try it ... **I AM Strong Girl ... I AM Strong Girl.**

– – – – – – – –

GOOD MORNING, STRONG GIRL.
WELCOME TO
Day Two

🚿 SAY IT: I am Strong Girl
God, help me to use the strength in you when I feel weak, help me to feel super-hero strong in my mind. Thank you for making me strong of mind and spirit with your words.
Amen.

PRAY IT: I am Strong Girl
He gives strength to the weary and increases the power of the weak.
Isaiah 40:29 (NIV)
The joy of the Lord will make you strong.
Nehemiah 8:10 ICB

It's easy to let things overwhelm you, however in tough times you have to stay strong. You must look for the positive. Keep the right attitude and you will quickly see just how strong you can be in any situation.
You are strong in mind, body and your spirit.

List 2-3 things that make you **strong.**

_____

_____

_____

With God, I'm better than I was yesterday, and I know my best days are in front of me.

GOOD MORNING, STRONG GIRL.
WELCOME TO
Day Three

 SAY IT: I am patient

God, help me to be patient and stay calm in all situations. When you are patient and keep a smile on your face you are growing in God and will learn to really enjoy life.
Amen.

 PRAY IT: I am patient

Better to be patient than powerful; better to have self-control than to conquer a city.
Proverbs 16:32 NLT

Act, don't react. Sometimes things just happen.
It's important to have patience and respond with the right attitude.
Sometimes you will be put into situations to test your patience.
Write down an example of where you have had to be patient and maybe write down a time when you weren't patient. What did you learn from it?

_____

_____

_____

_____

Pass the test. Be Patient.

GOOD MORNING, STRONG GIRL.
WELCOME TO
Day four

 SAY IT: I am energetic

God, I'm all yours! Thank you for helping me to use the energy you give me to be my best.
Amen.

 PRAY IT: I am energetic

I'm going to use all my energy, talents and skills for you!
1 Corinthians 10:31

Even if I am tired, I am Strong Girl and I get up and get my energy going. I eat right, I get plenty of rest, and get plenty of activity.

What are some things or activities that you do to keep your energy up? What time do you go to bed?

_____

_____

_____

_____

I can do all things through Christ because he gives me strength.
Philippians 4:13 (ICB)

Lessons Learned

I am beautiful. I am beautiful. I am beautiful.

When you see celebrities or pictures of models all with the same body type, it's easy to think that is what normal looks like. But what is normal? Whose definition of normal are you using? How about using your own definition of normal, or how about real?

The world is filled with people of all sizes and all shapes and everyone in their own way is beautiful. Celebrate your kind, silly, quirky, crazy, fun, unique you. This is who you are, this is how you were made, so celebrate your real, unique inner beauty. Beauty is really on the inside looking out! And Strong Girls embrace who they are.

Focus on being healthy. Wear clothes that make you feel good about yourself. Get plenty of rest and exercise, as this is what drives your healthy attitude. I have learned over the years that when I focus on how I feel, instead of what a scale or a number might say, I all of the sudden feel amazing.

I also surround myself with positive people who make me feel good, because they feel good. Most importantly, push this message of the new beauty to other girls. When you feel good, pay that feeling forward to your friends and family. I can't think of any reason not to!

GOOD MORNING, STRONG GIRL.
WELCOME TO
Day five

 SAY IT: I am beautIful

God, help me to see myself the way You see me. God you made me just the way I am, thank you for making me a beautiful child of God. Thank you that I am a masterpiece!
Amen.

 PRAY IT: I am energetic

So we have come to know and to believe the love that God has for us. God is love, and whoever abides in love abides in God, and God abides in him.
1 John 4:16

Why fit in when you were born to stand out?" -Dr. Suess

You have a beautiful smile, you have a beautiful personality, you have beautiful eyes, and you have beautiful hair. You, Strong Girl, have a beautiful heart! What makes you different, what makes you stand out, **MAKES you beautiful.**

Let's list 2 or 3 things you think are beautiful about you.

_____

_____

_____

_____

GOOD MORNING, STRONG GIRL. WELCOME TO
Day Six

 SAY IT: I am smart
God, help me to develop, grow, and show all the ways you have created me to be me. Thank you for making me a sponge to soak up all the things you want to teach me.
Amen.

 PRAY IT: I am smart
And let us not grow weary of doing good, for in due season we will reap, if we do not give up.
Galatians 6:9

I take the time to study hard and make sure I do my homework daily.

Smart is pretty, Smart is confident, Smart is you!

Keep in mind Strong Girl, you can't be a Smart Cookie if you have a crumbly attitude!

List two things you are doing to learn and grow.

_____

_____

_____

GOOD MORNING, STRONG GIRL.
WELCOME TO
Day Seven

 SAY IT: I am a friend

God, help me to be a friend to all, and to be slow to get angry with my friends. God, help me to not get angry with myself as well. Thank you for helping me to use my words to serve and bless others with kindness and thoughtfulness for I am a friend.
Amen.

 PRAY IT: I am a friend

But you, O Lord, are a God merciful and gracious, slow to anger and abounding in steadfast love and faithfulness.
Psalm 86:15

Strong Girls look for opportunities to be a friend to others. Have lunch at school with someone new. Say hi to someone new. Smile at someone new.

How can you be a friend to someone who **needs a friend?**

_____

_____

_____

_____

_____

Lessons Learned

About Honesty

A few days ago, this boy I know had somehow ruined his Pokémon cards. Since his cards were ruined, he asked me if I could help him get new ones. I said yes, because I wanted him to be my friend, and I wanted him to like me. So I asked my other friends if they could give me some Pokémon cards because I was starting my own collection. I ended up lying to a lot of my friends just to get free cards for this boy so he would be my friend. I wasn't thinking straight I guess.

I felt bad about it and ended up talking to my mom and dad about it. I decided that I would go purchase more Pokémon cards with the money I saved doing chores. With the new cards I bought, I made sure my friends got new ones in place of the ones I had gotten from them.

This whole Pokémon issue was a great lesson for me. From now on I am going to be honest. I don't need to impress people for them to be my friend. I didn't like the way it made me feel.

Love,
D.S.

GOOD MORNING, STRONG GIRL.
WELCOME TO
Day eight

SAY IT: I am honest

God, help me to be honest in all that I do. Because at the end of the day it is the best way to always honor you. Thank you for teaching me honesty and truth.
Amen.

PRAY IT: I am honest

"And you will know the truth, and the truth will set you free."
John 8:32

Being honest is the right thing to do. Sometimes we will make mistakes, however, it's important to be honest about our mistakes and take responsibility for them.

If it's not right, don't do it.
If it's not true, don't say it!
Be true to yourself, keep honesty first place.

Have you ever felt bad when you weren't honest? How did it make you feel?

_____

_____

_____

I learn from my mistakes.

GOOD MORNING, STRONG GIRL.
WELCOME TO
Day nine

SAY IT: I am talented
God, help me to continue to grow in my talents with practice, practice, practice. Thank you for creating me with special talents that I will continue to use in amazing ways.
Amen.

PRAY IT: I am talented
I can do all things through him who strengthens me.
Philippians 4:13

I can do anything I set my mind to.

If I practice, practice, and practice some more, and add in some hard work and imagination, the possibilities are limitless.

What **do** you love to do? What specials talents do you have?

_____

_____

_____

_____

GOOD MORNING, STRONG GIRL.
WELCOME TO
Day Ten

 SAY IT: I am happy

God, help me to understand that I always have a choice to be happy and to enjoy every day of my life. Thank you for helping me to think about things that are pure and lovely.

Amen.

 PRAY IT: I am happy

God made this day and I'm going to enjoy it and be happy.
Psalm 118:24

Did you know a smile is the best makeup any girl can wear? Smile often and turn that frown upside down Strong Girl!

Ah, perfect, and oh how beautiful you are!

What makes you happy?

_____

_____

_____

_____

time to check in!

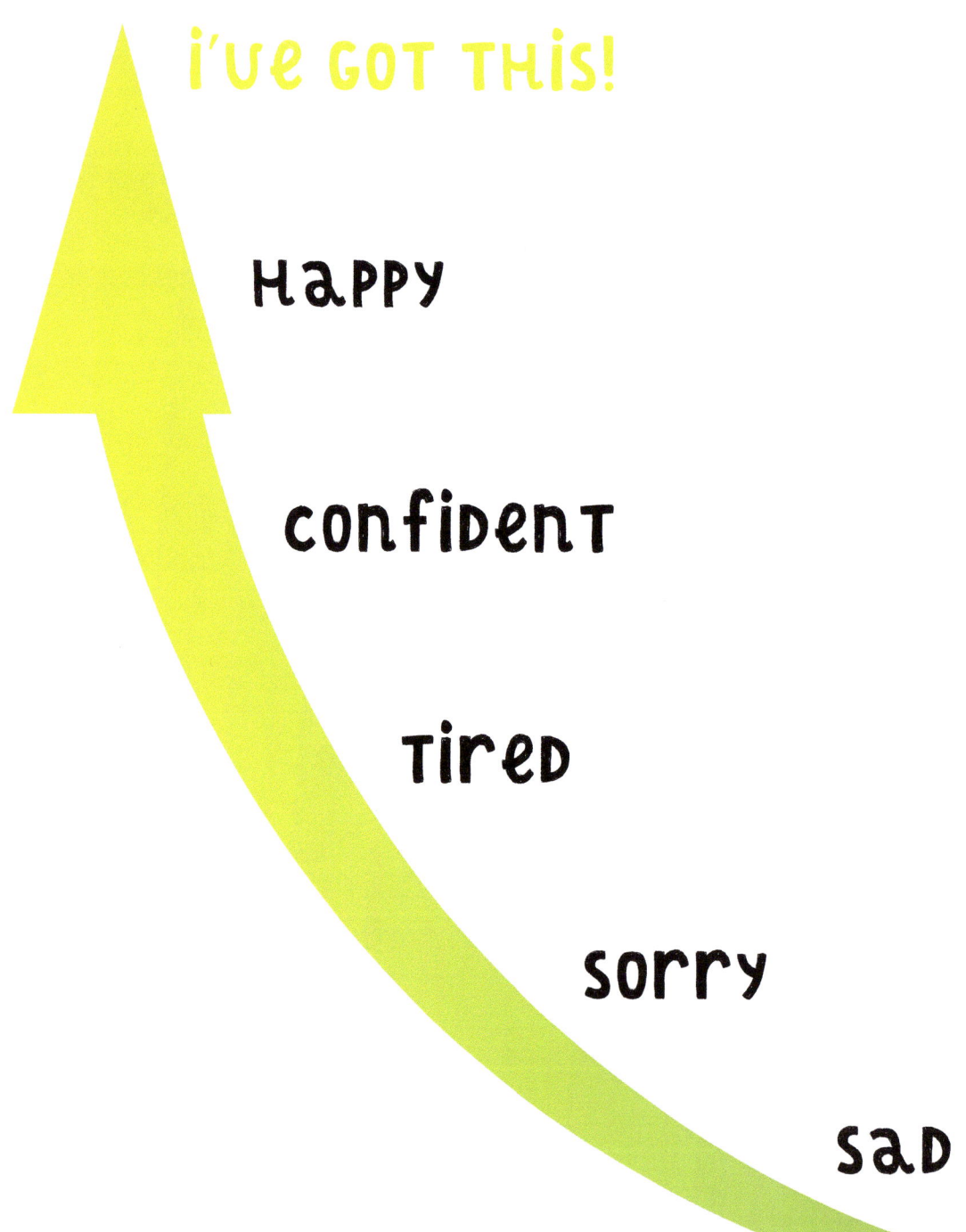

i've got this!

happy

confident

tired

sorry

sad

Circle how you are feeling right now. If you're in the bottom of the curve decide how you will climb to the top. With God on your side, you've got this, Strong Girl!

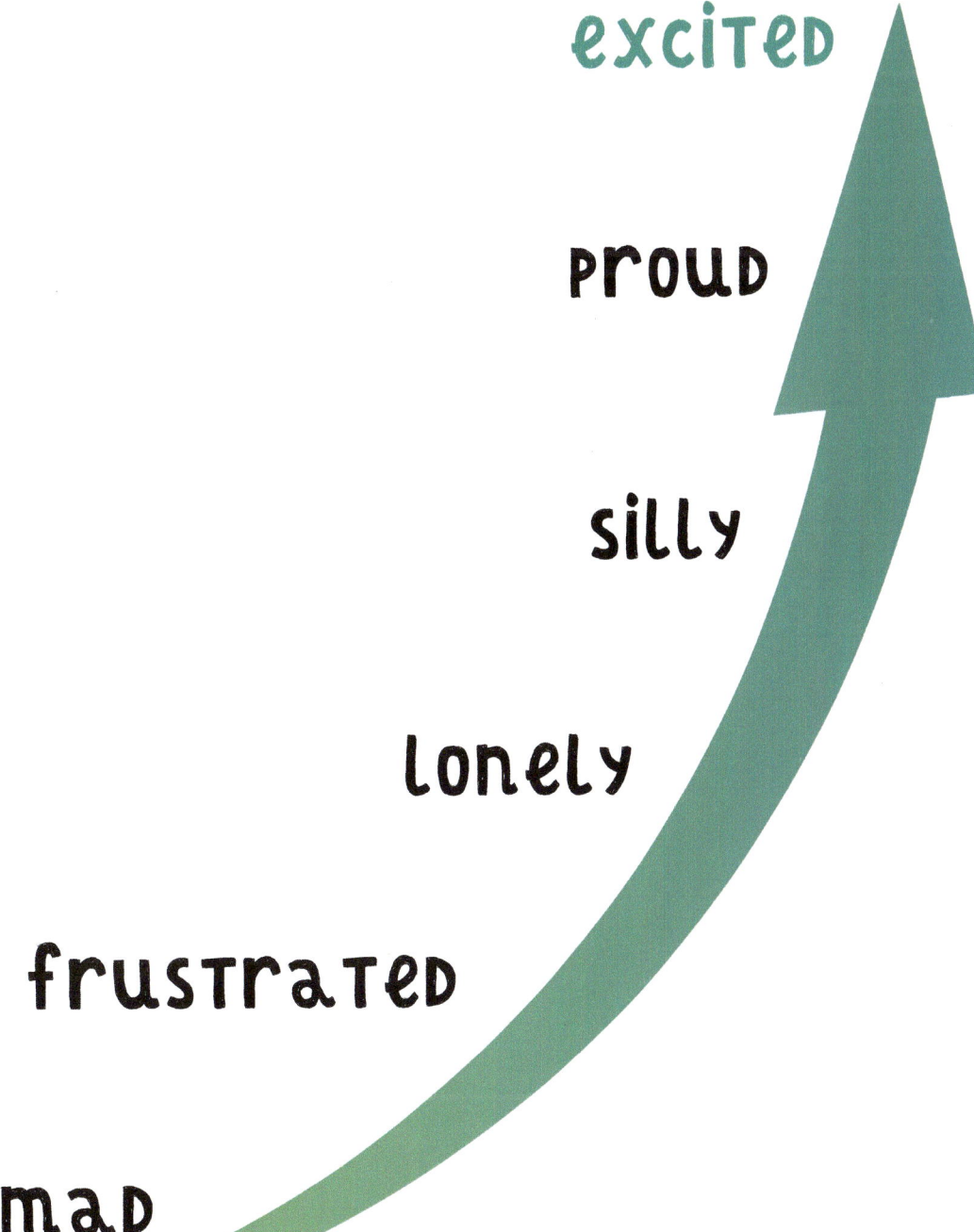

excited

proud

silly

lonely

frustrated

mad

Lessons Learned

Being healthy.

If you are going to be your best, you must keep your energy up. If you are going to keep your energy up, you must be healthy. How do I do that, you ask? Get outside and play. Breathe in some fresh air and get some sunshine. Get plenty of rest, and if you are to get plenty of rest, you need to get to bed at a decent time. Strong Girl, that means 7-8 hours of sleep each night. You know when Mom or Dad tells you that you need your rest ... well guess what? They are right!

Exercise is important and it's as easy as getting in a walk, a run, swimming, jump roping, playing hopscotch, hula hooping, or getting outside to play. I bet you can come up with many other ways to get in some activity each day. When I was growing up I loved to skip. As a matter of fact, I still love to skip, it's fun!

"With God, I'm better than I was yesterday, and I know my best days are in front of me."

GOOD MORNING, STRONG GIRL.
WELCOME TO
Day eleven

💧 SAY IT: I am healthy

God, help me get the proper rest so I am ready for the next wonderful day ahead of me. God, help me to take good care of myself so I can grow in body and mind. Thank you for helping me keep my healthy focus.
Amen.

PRAY IT: I am healthy

Dear friend, I pray that you may enjoy good health and that all may go well with you, even as your soul is getting along well.
3 John 1:2 (NIV)

I make healthy food choices to fuel my body. Healthy and strong is pretty.

Being healthy is important, however your worth is NOT determined by your body weight. Your worth is determined by who you are!

To be the best you can be, eat right, stay active, and get your sleep. Moving your body churns out good feelings and helps with positive seeds of strength. Your only limit is you!

What did you do today to be healthy?

_____

_____

_____

Lessons Learned

I am kind.

Sometimes kindness can be difficult. Sometimes we can be in a bad mood and not want to be kind. The real story here, Strong Girl, is that when we are unkind to our friends, family, or others, it's usually because we are not kind to ourselves.

To be kind to others, you must first start off by being kind to yourself. While this may be a different way to think about kindness, it is very important to start by being kind to yourself. Maybe you give yourself a big hug, or tell yourself a few times, "I am kind, I am kind, I am kind." Take a look in the mirror and tell yourself how amazing you are and how happy you are, even if you aren't happy in the moment. Just saying it will make it so, trust me! How about looking at some flowers or a tree or anything that just makes you smile. When you are kind to yourself, your kindness will spread to others around you, and that can start a movement of kindness everywhere.

GOOD MORNING, STRONG GIRL.
WELCOME TO
Day Twelve

🔔 SAY IT: I am kind

God, help me to be kind, to do something good for someone else and to share what I have, just as you do. Thank you for the kindness you always show me.
Amen.

PRAY IT: I am kind

Do not neglect to do good and to share what you have, for such sacrifices are pleasing to God.
Hebrews 13:16

What can you do today **to be kind to you?**

_____

_____

What can you do today **to be kind to someone else?**

_____

_____

GOOD MORNING, STRONG GIRL.
WELCOME TO
Day Thirteen

SAY IT: I am thankful

God, help me to be thankful for my family and friends and let me be kind to everyone around me. I will rise and shine and be thankful. Thank you for helping me to be grateful in everything.
Amen.

 PRAY IT: I am thankful

In the morning, Lord, you, hear my voice; in the morning I lay my requests before you and wait expectantly.
Psalm 5:3

Thanksgiving is not the only time of year I should be thankful.

Every day I am thankful for the little things and the big things. I am thankful for my mom, my dad, and my family. I am thankful for the sunshine, I am thankful for the rain, I am thankful for my warm bed, and I am thankful for my favorite books.

Now it's your turn. **What are you thankful for?**

_____

_____

_____

_____

GOOD MORNING, STRONG GIRL.
WELCOME TO
Day fourteen

SAY IT: I am courageous

God, help me to be courageous today and everyday and deal with fear head on. Thank you that I will not be afraid and I will be courageous with you in my life.
Amen.

🕊 PRAY IT: I am courageous

Lord, You are my shield...my wonderful God who gives me courage.
Psalm 3:3 ICB

Did you know Strong Girl, that this too shall pass and you **will** get past the tough bumps and hiccups of life and be much stronger because you were **courageous**?

How are you courageous?

_____

_____

_____

_____

_____

Lessons Learned

Encourager Activity

You are an encourager, not just for yourself, but for your friends, your family, your brother, and your sister. What can you do today to encourage someone?

_____

(Fill out the below section at the end of the day.)

Who did you encourage?

_____

What did you do to encourage them?

_____

How did it make them feel?

_____

How did it make you feel?

_____

GOOD MORNING, STRONG GIRL.
WELCOME TO
Day fifteen

 SAY IT: I am an encourager

God, help me when I am sad or feel down, so that I can become an encourager with your words to myself and others. Thank you for helping me to act, speak, and think so that I draw others toward you.
Amen.

 PRAY IT: I am an encourager

This is my comfort in my affliction, that your word has
revived me and given me life.
Psalm 119:50

I encourage my family and friends with positive thoughts and love.
Everybody has seeds of strength, sometimes I just have
to help them plant some.

What are some ways you can encourage yourself?

_____

_____

_____

_____

_____

GOOD MORNING, STRONG GIRL.
WELCOME TO
Day Sixteen

SAY IT: I am a learner

God, help me to learn your Word and know how to apply it to situations that happen in my life everyday. Thank you that I am learning to be strong in your word.
Amen.

PRAY IT: I am a learner

Always remember what is written in the Book of the Teachings. Study it day and night. Then you will be sure to obey everything that is written there. If you do this, you will be wise and successful in everything.
Joshua 1:8 (ICB)

I love to learn about new things.
Learning helps me grow, learning helps me be the best me I can be.

Learning is fun! Learning is cool!
What did I learn new today?

_____

_____

_____

_____

Lessons Learned

Joyful Activity

Being joyful is important, and it is also important to spread joyfulness to others. What can you do today, at school, at playtime, at home to spread joy? List one or two things you will do to bring joy to someone else.

_____

(Answer the questions below at the end of the day.)

What you did to spread joy?

_____

List how you felt spreading joy.

_____

List how that person/s felt when you were spreading the joy.

_____

List a way you can practice daily joyfulness.

_____

time to check in!

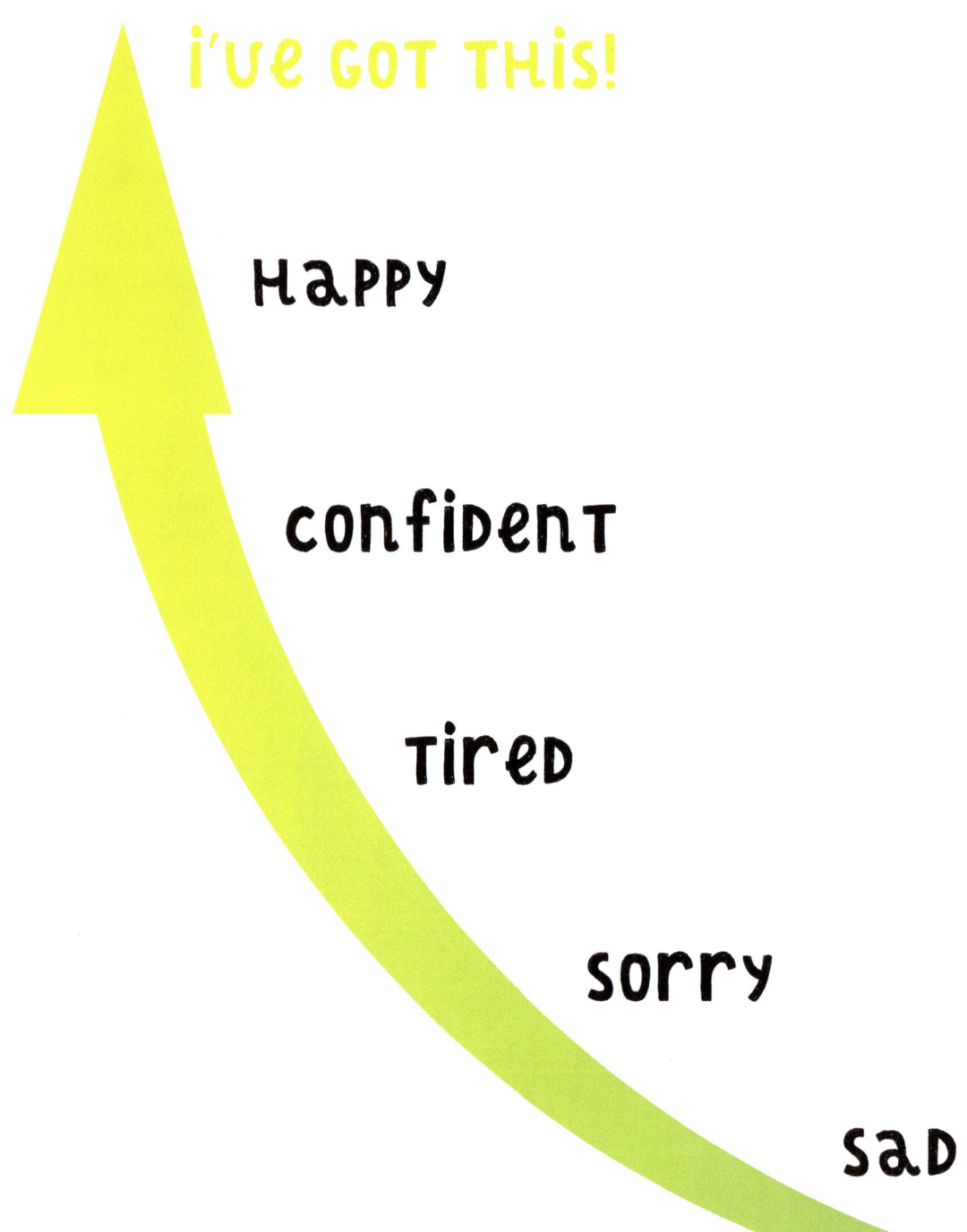

i've got this!

happy

confident

tired

sorry

sad

Circle how you are feeling right now. If you're in the bottom of the curve decide how you will climb to the top. With God on your side, you've got this, Strong Girl!

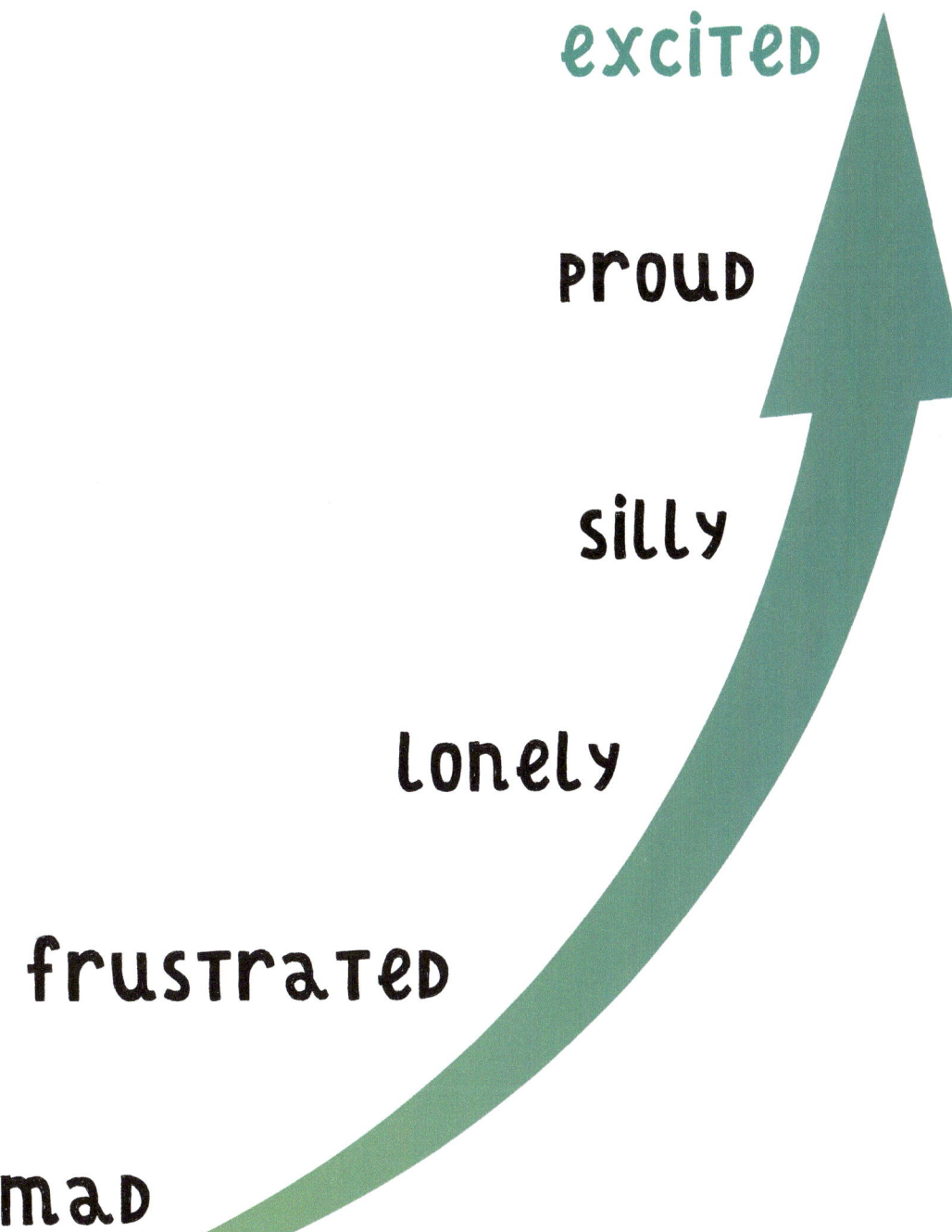

GOOD MORNING, STRONG GIRL. WELCOME TO
Day Seventeen

 SAY IT: I am joyful

God, today help be to be joyful in all I do and to be excited about all the things that will come my way. Thank you for giving me appreciation and Joy for others and all that they do.
Amen.

 PRAY IT: I am joyful

These things I have spoken to you, that my joy may be in you, and that your joy may be full.
John 15:11

I love to have fun, I love to laugh. I **will** laugh more often. Why not? Laughing and being full of joy is good for your mind, your heart and your body.

Being joyful is a choice. I choose to be joyful!

What are some fun/joyful things you like to do with your friends and family?

_____

_____

_____

_____

Lessons Learned

Being Excellent (by Ry)

I am excellent in all I do.
I am excellent in all I do.
I am excellent in all I do.

Here's what I did to start being excellent:
Today I made my life plan board. I put all of my life goals on the life plan board, like people I want to meet, things I want to do, and places I want to go. I also put projects coming up and my schedule for soccer. This will help me to be organized and I won't miss anything or come unprepared. That's being excellent!

I really love my life board, it's the BEST! I just wanted to share with Grandma and your readers. You have inspired me to be my best. Thank you and love you!

Hugs and kisses,
Ry

GOOD MORNING, STRONG GIRL.
WELCOME TO
Day eighteen

🕯️ SAY IT: I am excellent in all I do

God, help me to be excellent in all I do and have a good attitude along the way. Thank you for watching over me and helping me to see more of you in all I do.
Amen.

PRAY IT: I am excellent in all I do

You are young, but do not let anyone treat you as if you were not important. Be an example.
I Timothy 4:12 ICB

The Lord watches over you...
Psalm 121:5 (NIV)

This doesn't mean you have to be the best at everything, it just means you try your hardest and give it your all. That's acting with **EXCELLENCE.**

What have you done today to be your best?

_____

_____

_____

_____

GOOD MORNING, STRONG GIRL.
WELCOME TO
Day nineteen

 SAY IT: I am in charge of how I feel

God, help me to empty all the bad stuff out of my head each day and be filled with your word. I am in charge of how I feel and I will plant daily seeds of positive words into my mind. Thank you for helping me to stop, drop, and roll the negative thoughts out of my head and replace them with positive ones.
Amen.

PRAY IT: I am in charge of how I feel

Do not be shaped by this world. Instead be changed within by a new way of thinking. Then you will be able to decide what God wants for you. And you will be able to know what is good and pleasing to God and what is perfect.
Romans 12:2 (ICB)

Take charge for how you are feeling, you have a choice,
so choose happiness.

Strong Girl, how are you feeling today?
If you are sad or bored, then what can **you do** to change that up?

_____

_____

_____

_____

GOOD MORNING, STRONG GIRL.
WELCOME TO
Day Twenty

 SAY IT: I am valuable

God, help me to stay on the right path and always remember that you have a plan for me and that I am valuable. Thank you for directing my everyday footsteps.
Amen.

 PRAY IT: I am valuable

Direct my footsteps according to your word…
Psalm 119:133 (NIV)

There is a STRONG GIRL inside of every girl, and yes, that means you too! Your value is not determined by what other people say, but rather by who God says YOU are!

Feeding yourself the daily seeds of positive strength helps you to build your value.

You are valuable, you are Strong Girl.

What are some things you tell yourself about your **value?**

_____

_____

_____

GOOD MORNING, STRONG GIRL.
CONGRATULATIONS YOU ARE ON
Day Twenty One

 SAY IT: I am proud of myself

God, help me to never give up and be proud that you are leading me to be my best self ever. Thank you for being on my side and helping me get better and better every day.
Amen.

 PRAY IT: I am proud of myself

And I am sure of this, that he who began a good work in you
will bring it to completion at the day of Jesus Christ.
Philippians 1:6

I did it! I can do it. And if I fail I will just get up and try again.

Be proud of yourself, Strong Girl. You have taken a big step in daily discovery by planting your seeds of strength with God.

What will you do next to keep your daily seeds of positivity watered and growing?

_____

_____

_____

_____

where are you now?

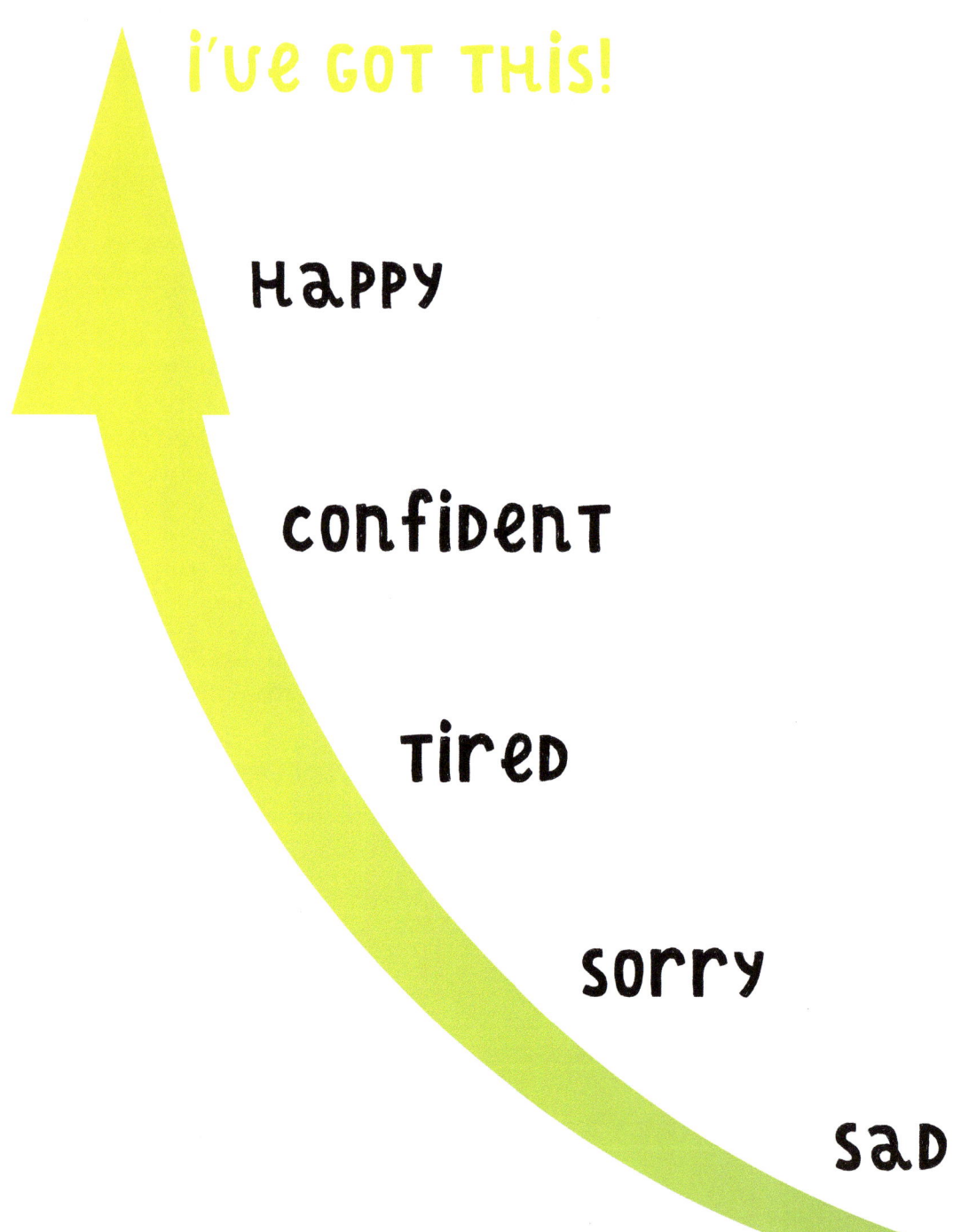

i've got this!

happy

confident

tired

sorry

sad

Circle how you are feeling right now. If you're in the bottom of the curve decide how you will climb to the top. With God on your side, you've got this, Strong Girl!

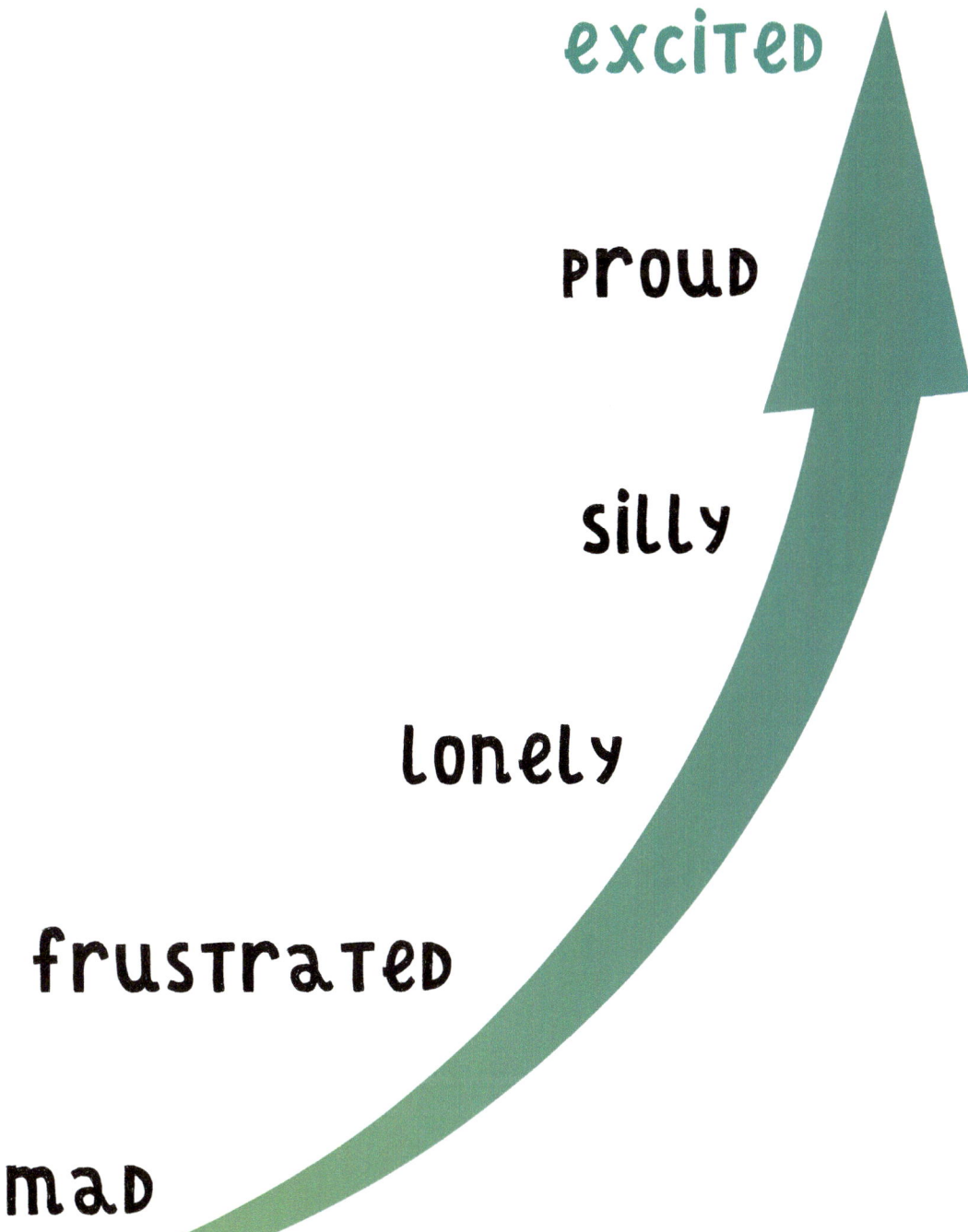

Lessons Learned

Write a Letter Activity

Write a letter to your older self and tell yourself how amazing, how wonderful, how excellent you will turn out. Say what it is you want to be in the future. After all, we become what we think about, so think big and be strong in your thinking. Here is my letter I wrote to myself when I was younger:

Dear Strong Girl,

I know sometimes life will be confusing to you. But I want you to stay strong and know that you are my hero. Whatever you might be going through is just part of growing up. Trust me, it will all work out, you must stay strong and love everything about you. You are beautiful, you are amazing, you are a bright light of confidence and love.

When life gets you down or things get to tough to stand, then kneel and pray because God is always listening. If for some reason you can t talk to Mom, Dad, your Brothers, or Friends, then know God is there for you. The more you talk things out with family, friends and God the more it all starts making sense. Life is full of bumps and bruises, so you must keep daily positive thoughts in front of you. You are Strong Girl and you will get past this stuff. Strong Girl you are awesome and even though you may not realize this right now, trust me, you will grow up and be a beautiful light of love, kindness, confidence, and strength! Life is good and you are never alone. Stay Strong my beautiful best friend! Go out and be AWESOME.

God Loves You and So Do I,
Your Younger Self

now it's your turn!
WRITE YOUR LETTER BELOW.

God knows just what to do.
Give your worries to the Lord. He will take care of you.
He will never let good people down.
PSALM 55:22 ICB

_____

_____

_____

_____

_____

_____

_____

_____

_____

About the Author

Terrie Nathan
Author & Strong Girl

TERRIE NATHAN is a #1 International Bestselling author, speaker and Confidence Strategist. Strong Girl Spirit with God is the second book in the Strong Girl Spirit Confidence Series. Terrie is the wife of a golf enthusiast, the mother of two amazing adult children, and grandma to three awesome grandchildren. She draws her inspiration, energy, and strength from her family and strong women, men, girls, and boys worldwide.

Her hope is to spread the message of faith and positive power across the world. Terrie and her husband, Eric, live in Virginia and enjoy all the outdoors activities the state has to offer. Terrie enjoys painting, pizza, and pineapple, and usually in that order, what a combination! Terrie and her family all share a passion for people and understand the importance of daily positive reinforcement in our lives and the lives of others.

Your words matter and so do you!
You DO make a difference.

Please share your positive stories regarding your seeds of strength!

VISIT terrienathan.com | EMAIL terrie@stronggirlspirit.com

@stronggirlspirit

@strong_girl_spirit

@stronggirl52

@stronggirl

www.ingramcontent.com/pod-product-compliance
Lightning Source LLC
Chambersburg PA
CBHW061402090426
42743CB00003B/121